Literary Paris

PHOTOGRAPHY AND COMMENTARY BY

JEFFREY KRAFT

WATSON-GUPTILL PUBLICATIONS

NEW YORK

⌐ *To Patrick, Pierre, my parents, and, always, to Frances* ¬

In my journey to publication I want to express my deep gratitude to all those who have wandered with me: Patrick Di Michele, Pierre Détraves, my parents Joyce and Jim Kraft, Dora and Robert Polatsek, Susan and Bob Jones, Richard Derus, Claudia Menza, Robin Simmen, Margaret Sobel, and Marian Appellof. My single greatest debt is to Frances, my partner, who shared every footpath and who, luckily for me, is also my wife. With apologies to Mrs. Wharton, each of you has had a hand in ensuring that these scenes will have been left to the few, not the indifferent.

Senior Editor: Robin Simmen
Developmental Editor: Marian Appellof
Editor: Margaret Sobel
Designer: Derek Bacchus
Production Manager: Ellen Greene

First published in the United States in 1999 by Watson-Guptill Publications,
a division of BPI Communications, Inc.,1515 Broadway, New York, N.Y. 10036

Library of Congress Cataloging-in-Publication Data
Kraft, Jeffrey F.
    Literary Paris / photography by Jeffrey F. Kraft.
        p.   cm.
    ISBN 0-8230-2830-5
1. Paris (France)–Pictorial works. 2. Paris (France)–In literature.   3. Literary landmarks–
France–Paris–Pictorial works. 4. Authors–France–Paris–Quotations. I. Title.
DC707.K69   1999
944'.36–dc21   99-10878
                                                                           CIP

Manufactured in Italy.

First printing, 1999

1 2 3 4 5 6 7 8 9 / 05 04 03 02 01 00 99

LITERARY PARIS

Contents

PLATE ONE: *Cour, Rue Vieille-du-Temple* 1992

À Propos

"The real voyage of discovery consists not in seeking new landscapes but in having new eyes."

MARCEL PROUST

Paris is, by turns, *grandeur* and *décadence,* strutting and fretting, Balzac and Proust.

While we are there it is the city of Balzac: a riot of sweeping panoramas peppered by taste, smell, and color. Its streets are awash with possibility, such that we are tempted and pushed forward by ornery Honoré to a point well past exhaustion. There's too much to describe, to capture, to wrestle to earth. So we just walk on, and marvel.

Yet in memory Paris is Proustian, a gradual unfolding backward. The spectacle somehow matters less than the actual windows through which we viewed it. Remember how French windows stand tall and full, with a spine and a reluctant knob so we can pull all of Paris—its horns, the scratch of a broom, dripping rain, a distant train—into our little rooms? How just beyond those windows lurk metal shutters, which, in another uniquely Parisian rite, let us open ourselves to the day's possibilities, then blot out the world at night, holding back our light from a city that needs none, steeling us against its damp, leaving us alone with our books or someone else or *madeleines?*

These photographs have less to do with Paris than with what it stirs within those of us who have spent time there. The city is forever a communion with the senses and a deeply personal journey; my challenge is to reconcile these. For someone who grew up in the American Midwest, as I did, Paris was first and necessarily an imagined place. In composing photographs I listen to the voices, the music, the din of *Paris éternel* from its vast trove of literature. Even as I came to know it, its writers remained the masters of Neverland, this Paris of our hearts. My hope is that image and text recreate for each reader an intimate or emotional moment within the attendant graces of a Parisian setting.

My choice of text is just that, my own. I am only a devoted student of French literature. Yet LITERARY PARIS is not intended as much for a reader as for the *flâneur,* that delightful (if not quite translatable) word used to describe an urban wanderer who observes with pause and interest. This is ultimately what Paris demands of each of us.

Panoramas

Paris demands to be seen from afar and at different angles, lovingly lit, coyly veiled. From any vantage point, even at first glance, this city is a *she.* But her splendor is so immense that we must scale an outer height or sink to the depth of the Seine to see her as she must first be seen: in relief and at somewhat of a distance.

Even today, little imagination is required to bear witness to Quasimodo's jagged bird's-eye perspectives or the poet Léon-Paul Fargue's jade broth of a river alive with tugboats. That these vistas have endured is no small miracle. It is this sense that I have tried to capture in this first group of images.

Imagined Paris lives up to reality. It fascinates me that she still rises up from memory, a Gray Lady, a monument to herself not easily altered or even repaired (as Janet Flanner so aptly noted). Many of these photos make the most of sudden light: layers of gray forced into contrast; true blackness etching sharper silhouettes.

The vantage points of these photos mirror that first mind's-eye view of the city we all share, thanks to her literary suitors through time. These are the moments we try to take in all that is Paris. And no matter how many years separate us from the panorama, we can go back in our minds and our hearts to that incomparable sight.

Panoramas

As admirable as Paris today might seem, recreate and rebuild in your mind the Paris of the fifteenth century, see daylight through an astonishing hedge formed of spires, towers, and steeples, filter through an immense city, tear away to the tips of its isles, fold into the arcs of the bridges spanning the Seine, its wide green and yellow pools as iridescent as snakeskin; place the Gothic profile of old Paris squarely against an azure horizon, cloak a winter mist 'round its many chimneys, then plunge it into nightfall and note the bizarre interplay of light and shade in this somber labyrinth of buildings, toss in a moonbeam to help highlight it, and raise the large heads of its towers from the fog; take this black silhouette, revived by the jagged shadows of spires and gables, and make it come alive, more crenellated than a shark's jaw, against the coppery sky of a sunset. — Then compare.

Victor Hugo	NOTRE-DAME DE PARIS	*1831*

PLATE TWO: *Au Sacré-Cœur* 1990

Panoramas

I thought I saw a black sun in the empty sky and a blood-red globe hanging over the Tuileries. I said to myself: "The eternal night is beginning, and it is going to be frightful. What will happen when men realize that there is no sun anymore?"

| Gérard de Nerval | AURÉLIA | 1855 |

PLATE THREE: *Soleil rouge, Saint-Sulpice* 1990

Panoramas

In the raw veiled spring morning faint odours float of morning Paris: aniseed, damp sawdust, hot dough of bread: and as I cross the Pont Saint Michel the steelblue waking waters chill my heart.

| *James Joyce* | NIGHTPIECE | *1915* |

PLATE FOUR: *Pont-Neuf* 1995

Panoramas

M y three-room apartment there opened onto a balcony with a commanding view of the Seine, one from which I could contemplate the gigantic monuments, Notre-Dame, Saint-Jacques-la-Boucherie, Sainte-Chapelle, etc. With the sky, water, air, swallows, and rooftop greenery I felt less a part of cultivated Paris, inappropriate to both my tastes and means, than the picturesque and poetic Paris of Victor Hugo, a city of the past.

George Sand	HISTOIRE DE MA VIE	*1855*

PLATE FIVE: *La Flèche, Notre-Dame* 1997

Panoramas

His European visits were infrequent enough to have kept unimpaired the freshness of his eye, and he was always struck anew by the vast and consummately ordered spectacle of Paris: by its look of having been boldly and deliberately planned as a background for the enjoyment of life, instead of being forced into grudging concessions to the festive instincts, or barricading itself against them in unenlightened ugliness, like his own lamentable New York.

| *Edith Wharton* | MADAME DE TREYMES | *1907* |

PLATE SIX: *Jardin des Plantes* 1997

Panoramas

Within Paris are streets as treacherous as any man guilty of betrayal; just as there are aristocratic streets, simple-but-honest streets, youthful streets whose morality has not yet been determined by the general public, murderous streets, streets older than even the oldest of dowagers, proper streets, streets that are ever clean, streets that are always filthy, working-class, studious, mercantile streets. Yes, the streets of Paris have human qualities, and impress upon us by their outward appearance certain perceptions against which we are defenseless.

Honoré de Balzac	FERRAGUS	*1833*

PLATE SEVEN: *Rue de Rivoli* 1995

Panoramas

A nd we sat in my room on the wide stone window seat, in an open gabled window that looked over the chimney pots of Paris, and ate the strawberries and cream, dipping each berry into the cream and feeding each other, and sadly watching the sun set over Paris.

| *Langston Hughes* | THE BIG SEA | *1940* |

PLATE EIGHT: *Silhouette, Passy* 1993

Panoramas

I watched the Eiffel Tower grow.

We all went to see it, after school, aprons still tied to our uniforms.

Parents marveled at its progress, like they were measuring their sons against a wall with a pencil.

The Seine, still rather placid then, played sadly with whatever came its way along a shoreline of pavilions, pomp and circumstance.

Tugs draped their heads on the river, with moans like a wounded ogress.

Tour boats netted in sunshine came and went like rays of honey.

It was a time when, whether he needed it or not, the Alma bridge's little soldier took his yearly bath all the way up to his belly.

| *Léon-Paul Fargue* | D'APRÈS PARIS | *1932* |

PLATE NINE: *La Tour à l'envers* 1995

Passages

aron Haussmann's pitiless urban overhaul in the mid-1800s wiped out most of the medieval maze, but Paris at least remains a labyrinth of the nineteenth century. How or what you go through, across, into, or under is one of the principal joys of any Paris journey. The winding staircases, the elevators, the quays, the dusty footpaths in the gardens, the ankle-turning *pavés* of the Latin Quarter, the anthill that is the Métro — are relentless and relentlessly unique.

The sense of smell, so visceral, goes wanting in photographs. Yet the nose, as Isak Dinesen points out, is memory. Everyday Paris scents like cheese, bread, cut flowers, and raw meat and fish create passages, sharpen our senses, and remind us that we often follow a mental path through this city even as we are exploring it visually.

In Paris there is always some byway in which to take cover, to wait, to sit, to sip. These photographs convey those places where we do stop, not only to rest or admire, but also to be introspective, where we can enjoy our own leaps of consciousness that the moment demands. Here at last is time to be sensitive, receptive. Léon-Paul Fargue knew that this allows us to discern murmurs — of memory, the grass, hinges, the dead. "One must become silent in order for silence to play her melodies, sad so that misery creeps our way," he wrote. "One waits so that the wait at last must be played out."

Passages

Idrank you and was left untouched

But I knew then how to savor the universe
I am reeling having drunk the whole universe
Along the waterfront where I saw waves lap and barges sleep

Hear me I am the maw of Paris
And I will drink the universe again if I wish

Listen to my songs of universal drunkenness

Then the September night slowly ended
The red lights of the bridges snuffed out in the Seine
The stars expiring Day was dawning again

Guillaume Apollinaire

"VENDÉMIAIRE" ALCOOLS

1913

PLATE TEN: *Le Pont et la Seine* 1995

Passages

J ust as there is no Parisian glance that is not compelled to encounter it, there is no fantasy that fails, sooner or later, to acknowledge its form and be nourished by it.

Roland Barthes	LA TOUR EIFFEL	*1964*

PLATE ELEVEN: *Détail de la Tour* 1992

Passages

A ll my life I have thought of France in a certain way. This is inspired by sentiment as much as by reason. The emotional side of me tends to imagine France, like the princess in the fairy stories or the Madonna in the frescoes, as dedicated to an exalted and exceptional destiny. Instinctively I have the feeling that Providence has created her either for complete successes or for exemplary misfortunes. If, in spite of this, mediocrity shows in her acts or deeds, it strikes me as an absurd anomaly, to be imputed to the faults of Frenchmen, not to the genius of the land. But the positive side of my mind also assures me that France is not really herself unless in the front rank; that only vast enterprises are capable of counter-balancing the ferments of dispersal that are inherent in her people; that our country, as it is, surrounded by others, as they are, must aim high and hold itself straight, on pain of mortal danger. In short, to my mind, France cannot be France without greatness.

| *Charles de Gaulle* | MÉMOIRES DE GUERRE: L'APPEL | *1954* |

PLATE TWELVE: *Au Louvre* 1995

Passages

I have always been lured by the hidden geography, by unique subject matter, also by shadows, sadness, premonitions, muffled steps, the suffering that crouches under doorways, smells both waiting and awaited, on one paw, ghosts passing, the reminiscences of old windows, scents, sudden movements, reflections, and the ashes of memory.

| *Léon-Paul Fargue* | LE PIÉTON DE PARIS | *1939* |

PLATE THIRTEEN: *À Passy* 1997

Passages

It is a solemn city of winding streets and of miniature marble temples and mansions of the dead gleaming white from out a wilderness of foliage and fresh flowers. Not every city is so well peopled as this or has so ample an area within its walls. Few palaces exist in any city that are so exquisite in design, so rich in art, so costly in material, so graceful, so beautiful.

| *Mark Twain* | THE INNOCENTS ABROAD | *1869* |

PLATE FOURTEEN: *Marches Père-Lachaise* 1993

Passages

The ancient stillness of the building stirred forgotten memories the brother and sister had of its blackened stones. They went up the stone staircase with deepening anxiety, and when the concierge had at last opened the door of the apartment, they remained at the entrance, afraid of entering these rooms where it seemed all their childhood memories had been stacked away, like little dead things.

| *Anatole France* | MONSIEUR BERGERET À PARIS | *1901* |

PLATE FIFTEEN: *Escalier, Vivienne* 1993

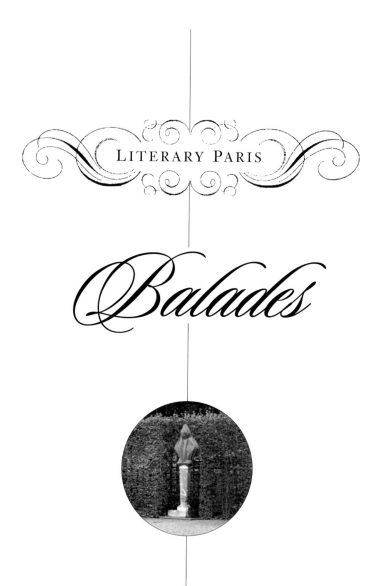

LITERARY PARIS

Balades

Despite all the outward graciousness, as the nostalgic French writer Francis Carco observed, Paris remains harder to grasp than to ignore. Happily it can be walked. And the single best way to set about understanding the city is just to get out and go—*faire une balade*—stopping wherever you please.

A *balade* is more a pilgrimage than a mere walk. Paris is for long, exploratory strolls—through her gardens, with their fat brown leaves, through courtyards, along grand boulevards and tiny, narrow streets—with your eyes wide open, taking in every detail. Such travels might find you gazing at the glistening slate of Notre-Dame as the sky clears after a cloudburst, admiring market stalls spilling over with produce, or sitting completely alone in a café in the early morning, watching the butter of your *tartine* melt in the hot milk of your coffee.

On a long-distance ramble, it's easy to stray beyond Paris proper into the Île de France, as some of these photographs do. Strictly urban landscapes give way to countryside, to the palaces and parks of Versailles and Vaux-le-Vicomte, and to roads less traveled. The desire for greenery is a natural one; Zola and Maupassant, among others, frequently pushed their characters beyond the city limits into rural cabarets and grassy stretches of the Seine. We take pause and breathe deeply in these expanses. The intensity of Paris recedes, if only for awhile. As readers or as travelers, we come to understand that *balades* are never so much plot devices as they are necessary changes in perspective.

Balades

So I say to you — this chateau in its shade
Held love, within your heart as fresh,
And glory, laughter, and myriad larks,
And all that joy now renders it dark,
Old liqueur staining a blackened vase.

Into this grotto, where moss covers stone,
Came, eyes down and breast beating,
A lovely Caussade or a young Candale,
Who, to a royal lover mere conquests feudal,
In coming called him Lord, then Louis in leaving.

Victor Hugo

"PASSÉ," LES VOIX INTERIORS

1837

PLATE SIXTEEN: *Vaux* 1993

Balades

The face of Paris is beautiful, but it loses in beauty when you know its true character. I always try to admire it plastically, regardless of its significance, but it is seldom that I can see the features without the spirit that lies behind them. Its coloring, its regularity, are perfect, but the expression is ugly.

| | *Anaïs Nin* | |

THE EARLY DIARY OF ANAÏS NIN,
VOLUME III: 1923-1927

PLATE SEVENTEEN: *L'Urne au Louvre* 1990

Balades

Where the sun fell all was hung with the mist as with a grey curtain of light. Grey in the grey, the statues sunned themselves in the not yet unshrouded gardens.

Rainer Maria Rilke

THE NOTEBOOKS OF
MALTE LAURIDS BRIGGE

1910

PLATE EIGHTEEN: *Au Grand Trianon* 1997

Balades

The young girl passed by,
quick and sprightly as a bird:
in her hand a shimmering bloom,
from her mouth a novel tune.

Perhaps the only one in the world
whose heart could answer mine,
and who, entering my deepest night
could enlighten it with a single look.

But no — my youth has gone
Farewell sweet ray that shone on me —
Scent, girl and song . . .
Happiness was passing by — It has fled.

Gérard de Nerval

"UNE ALLÉE DU LUXEMBOURG" ODELETTES

1832

PLATE NINETEEN: *État de Grace* 1993

Balades

Oh melancholy perfume of dead leaves which in the gardens, in the autumn, evoke the memory of extinguished lives . . . Sad and funereal charm, under which death would seem sweet, mixed with all that goes away and says to us adieu. . . .

| *Odilon Redon* | À SOI-MÊME | *1922* |

PLATE TWENTY: *Feuilles mortes* 1993

Balades

Versailles is a borough of Paris, yet it is decidedly not Paris. That is the question. To be and not to be in Paris.

	Arthur Rimbaud	

LETTRE DU BARON DE PETDECHÈVRE À SON
SECRÉTAIRE AU CHÂTEAU DE SAINT-MAGLOIRE

1871

PLATE TWENTY-ONE: *Fenêtre sur cour* 1992

Balades

Then we sat in silence for awhile, smoking cigarettes, surrounded by oyster shells, and finishing the wine. I was all at once very tired. I looked out into the narrow street, this strange, crooked corner where we sat, which was brazen now with the sunlight and heavy with people — people I would never understand.

James Baldwin	GIOVANNI'S ROOM	*1956*

PLATE TWENTY-TWO:  *Aperçu, Quartier Saint-Sulpice* 1990

Balades

I can hear the glass door of the *café* grate on the sand as I open it. I can recall the smell of every hour. In the morning that of eggs frizzling in butter, the pungent cigarette, coffee and bad cognac; at five o'clock the fragrant odour of absinthe; and soon after the steaming soup ascends from the kitchen; and as the evening advances, the mingled smells of cigarettes, coffee, and weak beer. A partition rising a few feet or more over the hats, separates the glass front from the main body of the *café*. The usual marble tables are there, and it is there we sat and aestheticized till two o'clock in the morning.

George Moore

CONFESSIONS OF A YOUNG MAN

1888

PLATE TWENTY-THREE: *Chaises empilées* 1990

Balades

It was an ocean! And it spread from Saint-Eustache church to Halles Road amid the two pavilions. From the outer edges of these crossroads the surf swelled higher, vegetables spilling over the cobblestones. Sunrise came gently, in a lovely pale gray, bathing the entire scene in watercolor tones. This river of greenery, fleecy stacks cresting like waves, seemed to flood the pavement hollows like the runoff from an autumn cloudburst.

| *Émile Zola* | LE VENTRE DE PARIS | *1873* |

PLATE TWENTY-FOUR: *Au Marché d'Aligre* 1997

Balades

After one love, another will begin

A little chap will come whistling along

Tomorrow,

His arms filled with spring

Marcel Achard

DEMAIN IL FERA JOUR *(Song of Edith Piaf)*

1951

PLATE TWENTY-FIVE: *Printemps, Marais* 1995

LITERARY PARIS

Lettres

The long-ago Paris in Eugène Atget's photographs teems with typefaces, ranging from gilded new signage to blackened words stretched across brick façades. Painted words, especially those faded and forgotten, have their private histories. Typography adds depth to topography.

Take Le Select in Montparnasse. The acid-green neon still coils around a street corner, the mere sight still evoking Hemingway and Jean Rhys and other literary rendezvous of the Lost Generation. Capucines, Bonne Nouvelle, République, and others — Métro stop names, spelled out on station walls — were whispered words of love to the poet Pierre Unik, who, before he died in 1945, recalled them as "all my history, all our music, humming like a chord."

Lettres

"Where do you want to go?" I asked. Brett turned her head away.

"Oh, go to the Select."

"Café Select," I told the driver. "Boulevard Montparnasse." We drove straight down, turning around the Lion de Belfort that guards the passing Montrouge trams. Brett looked straight ahead. On the Boulevard Raspail, with the lights of Montparnasse in sight, Brett said: "Would you mind very much if I asked you to do something?"

"Don't be silly."

"Kiss me just once more before we get there."

| *Ernest Hemingway* | THE SUN ALSO RISES | *1926* |

PLATE TWENTY-SIX: *Montparnasse, 11h du soir* 1990

Lettres

An atmosphere of departed and ephemeral loves hung about the bedroom like stale scent, for the hotel was one of unlimited hospitality, though quietly, discreetly and not more so than most of its neighbours. The wallpaper was vaguely erotic—huge and fantastically shaped mauve, green and yellow flowers sprawling on a black ground. There was one chair and a huge bed covered with a pink counterpane. It was impossible, when one  looked at that bed, not to think of the succession of *petites femmes* who had extended themselves upon it, clad in carefully thought out pink or mauve chemises, full of tact and savoir faire and savoir vivre and all the rest of it.

| *Jean Rhys* | QUARTET | *1929* |

PLATE TWENTY-SEVEN: *L'Hôtel* 1993

Lettres

F amiliarity does not breed contempt. On the contrary the more familiar it is the more rare and beautiful it is. Take the quarter in which one lives, it is lovely, it is a place rare and beautiful and to leave it is awful.

I remember once hearing a conversation on the street in Paris and it ended up, and so there it was there was nothing for them to do, they had to leave the quarter. There it was, there was nothing else to do they had to leave the most wonderful place in the world, wonderful because it was there where they had always lived.

Paris quarters were like that, we all had our quarters, to be sure when later we left them and went back to them they did look dreary, not at all like the lovely quarter in which we are living now. So familiarity did not breed contempt.

| *Gertrude Stein* | PARIS FRANCE | *1940* |

PLATE TWENTY-EIGHT: *Rue Jacob* 1990

Lettres

Poor street that will not that can not speak
   poor stripped-bare, underfed street
they took the bread from your mouth

ripped away your womb

cut the grass from under your feet

forced your songs back down your throat

stripped away your gladness

and the sparkle in your laughter broke its teeth

on an iron curtain of stupidity and hate

Jacques Prévert

"LA RUE DE BUCI MAINTENANT. . ."
PAROLES

1948

PLATE TWENTY-NINE: *Condamné* 1993

Lettres

You! Bear witness that I did my duty
Like a brilliant chemist, like a sainted soul.
For from each thing I extracted the quintessence,
You gave me your muck and I turned it to gold.

Charles Baudelaire

LES FLEURS DU MAL (EPILOGUE)

1861

PLATE THIRTY: *Au Marais* 1995

LITERARY PARIS

Lumières

"The sun doesn't get up very high, but the skies have been clear every day. The sunsets are spectacular: a gradual dimming of light with the sky changing from lavender to mauve, then pinkening. The rooftops, chimneys, and pigeons etch a sharp silhouette against it as it fades toward black."

These words—my own—were on the back of a postcard sent from Paris. It is never truly dark there, nor ever truly light. I recall writing the postcard, but not seeing the actual sun at dawn or sunset. Perhaps it is because the city glows, lit from within. Daylight infuses her *vieilles pierres* with a radiance that seems almost human. The evening light then arrives gently golden with a quality akin to magnified candlelight. Even indoor light seems kind. Whether refracted through stained glass or cracked panes, daylight neither overwhelms nor is overwhelmed by the incandescent.

The Eiffel Tower was reilluminated more than a decade ago, but the nighttime effect still amazes. Prior to its centennial, in 1989, the tower rose up at night like a ghost trapped in headlights. Then the lights were repositioned from the banks of the Seine to within the structure itself. That single act transformed the tower into a jewel; steel and rivets became an endless series of facets splintering the interior light.

Grace, our elder daughter, could not take her eyes off this shimmering finger floating above the tree line of the Champ-de-Mars. Each evening she pointed it out in silent wonder and smiled, knowing its appearance indicated that we were almost home. She was just learning to speak at the time, so it's still no small source of personal pride that a primitive pronunciation of Eiffel Tower ranked among her first words.

Lumières

O ne dies for a cathedral. Not for its stones. One dies for a people. Not for a mob. One dies for the love of a Man, if he is the keystone of a Community. One dies for only that which one can live for.

Antoine de Saint-Exupéry | PILOTE DE GUERRE | *1942*

PLATE THIRTY-ONE: *Saint-Eustache* 1997

Lumières

A breath of Paris preserves the soul.

Victor Hugo	LES MISÉRABLES	*1862*

PLATE THIRTY-TWO: *Lustres, Palais-Royal* 1993

Lumières

Oh! To wander Paris! Such a lovely, delectable experience! Strolling is a science, gastronomy for the eye. To walk is merely to exist, strolling is living.

Honoré de Balzac | LA PHYSIOLOGIE DU MARIAGE | *1829*

PLATE THIRTY-THREE: *La Fontaine, Palais-Royal* 1993

Lumières

At any season, and all year long, in the evening the view of the city from the bridges was always exquisitely pictorial. One's eyes became the eyes of a painter, because the sight itself approximated art, with the narrow, pallid façades of the buildings lining the river; with the tall trees growing down by the water's edge; with, behind them, the vast chiaroscuro of the palatial Louvre, lightened by the luminous lemon color of the Paris sunset off toward the west; with the great square, pale stone silhouette of Notre-Dame to the east. The stance from which to see Paris was any one of its bridges at the close of the day.

Janet Flanner	PARIS WAS YESTERDAY	*1972*

PLATE THIRTY-FOUR: *Pont Alexandre* III 1995

Lumières

An odd light dominates the assortment of covered arcades that abound in Paris within reach of the main boulevards which are rather disturbingly called *passages,* as if no one had the right to pause in these light-starved corridors for more than an instant. A glaucous sheen, as if seen through deep water, like the sudden brightness of a leg revealed beneath a lifted skirt.

| Louis Aragon | LE PAYSAN DE PARIS | 1926 |

PLATE THIRTY-FIVE: *À la Galerie Vivienne* 1995

Lumières

I therefore will not pretend to have been looking at Paris with new eyes, or to have gathered on the banks of the Seine a harvest of extraordinary impressions. I will only pretend that a good many old impressions have recovered their freshness, and that there is a sort of renovated entertainment in looking at the most brilliant city in the world with eyes attuned to a different pitch.

Henry James | PORTRAITS OF PLACES | *1883*

PLATE THIRTY-SIX: *L'Aube sur la Seine* 1995

Lumières

Those who have not admired your dark landscapes, bursts of light, deep and silent dead ends, nor heard your rumblings in the wee hours, know nothing of true poetry or of your strange and abundant contrasts.

| *Honoré de Balzac* | FERRAGUS | *1833* |

PLATE THIRTY-SEVEN: *À l'ombre* 1997

Lumières

A mauve sky, which the illuminations filled with something like the glow of an enormous fire — [. . .] the Eiffel Tower looking like a beacon left behind on earth by a vanished generation, a generation of men ten cubits tall.

Edmond and Jules de Goncourt

JOURNAL DES GONCOURT: MÉMOIRES
DE LA VIE LITTÉRAIRE

6 May 1889

PLATE THIRTY-EIGHT: *Feux, Tour Eiffel* 1990

Lumières

B ut Paris was a very old city and we were young and nothing was simple there, not even poverty, nor sudden money, nor the moonlight, nor right and wrong nor the breathing of someone who lay beside you in the moonlight.

| *Ernest Hemingway* | A MOVEABLE FEAST | *1964* |

PLATE THIRTY-NINE: *Pleine Lune* 1997

Solitaire

We all can remember spending the last day in a place we never want to leave. The first time I had to leave Paris after living there for an extended time still haunts me. I was completely alone that day, but not at all in a sorrowful way.

I had walked to catch a showing of *Les Enfants du paradis* at the vintage Ranelagh movie palace on a wet Sunday in late September. The actors and the poetry of Jacques Prévert's screenplay made me so wistful for nineteenth-century Paris that I decided to walk home that night, in a downpour. The streets were empty. A cold rain sliced down in sheets the entire way back. My route carried me over Apollinaire's soulful Pont Mirabeau, then up the narrow Allée des Cygnes to the Pont de Bir-Hakeim. I vividly recall squinting in the yellow lights to find my way, the black Seine on either side of me. I have rarely felt more alive.

I find something of the wondrous solitary feeling of that day in these photos. They pair well with some favorite literary passages — especially the selection from Colette and the epic close of Balzac's masterpiece, *Le Père Goriot.* Each is a still life of a quintessential Parisian scene and the commemoration of a scent, a touch, or a moment alone.

Solitaire

Thinking, dreaming, conceiving great works, is a delightful pastime. It's like smoking magic cigars or living the life of a kept woman who thinks only of her own pleasure. Work is in its state of infant grace, living out the simple joys of a new generation, dressed in pale floral colors, like juice swiftly suckled before the fruit has even been eaten. Such is the act of Conception and its related joys. The person who paints with words is immediately thought to be an extraordinary individual. All artists and writers have mastered this. But then produce! Go into labor! Raise the child, sending it off to bed every night gorged with milk, licking it clean when it's dirty, dressing it hundreds of times in beautiful playclothes that get torn to shreds; how not to be disheartened by all the turmoil of this mad existence and somehow create a living masterpiece that appeals to all seers of sculpture, all cognoscenti of literature, all nostalgics for painting, all lovers of music, such is Production and its labors. A hand able to move at a moment's notice, ready within the fraction of a second to obey the brain. Yet the brain is unable to command the creative faculty, as inconstant as love.

Honoré de Balzac | LA COUSINE BETTE | *1847*

PLATE FORTY: *Buste, Palais-Garnier* 1989

Solitaire

————|—————————————|————

Standing before this woman in this salon furnished like so many others in the Saint-Germain district with rich hobnobs draped across tables, admiring its books and cut flowers, he felt ensconced in Paris. Sinking into a true Parisian carpet, he rediscovered the singular mold, the delicate shapes, of the Parisienne, her flawless grace and casual nonchalance of these desired effects. . . .

Honoré de Balzac | LA FEMME ABANDONNÉE | *1833*

PLATE FORTY-ONE: 1990

Solitaire

From the open windows the air that had not slept last night crept out with a bad conscience.

Rainer Maria Rilke	THE NOTEBOOKS OF MALTE LAURIDS BRIGGE	*1910*

PLATE FORTY-TWO: *À Belleville* 1997

Solitaire

And so on that day, in that glorious hour, the homely, inexpensive chair belonging to the municipality of Paris became the empty throne which is always beseeching the restless spirit of man to end his fear and longing and proclaim the kingdom of man.

| *Henry Miller* | THE WISDOM OF THE HEART | *1941* |

PLATE FORTY-THREE: *Banos* 1997

Solitaire

He didn't answer, driven by his impending pleasure and the desire to have her again. She complied and was a good mistress, attentive and serious, to her young lover. Yet she endured him like a penance, pushing him away with feeble hands while holding him fast with her powerful knees. She finally grabbed him by the arms, cried out weakly, and plunged into the abyss from which love emerges, pale, mute and full of regret for its death.

Colette	CHÉRI	*1920*

PLATE FORTY-FOUR: *L'Instant* 1995

Solitaire

Whoever looks through an open window from outside never sees as much as the one who gazes upon a closed window. No object is deeper, more mysterious, more fertile, more shadowy, more amazing, than a window lit by a candle. Whatever can be seen in daylight is always less interesting than what happens on the opposite side. For inside this black or ill-lit hole life lives, life dreams, life suffers.

Charles Baudelaire | "LA FENÊTRE" PETITS POÈMES EN PROSE | *1869*

PLATE FORTY-FIVE: *En face* 1993

Solitaire

She felt a little betrayed and sad, but presently a moving object came into sight. It was a huge horse-chestnut tree in full bloom bound for the Champs Élysées, strapped now into a long truck and simply shaking with laughter—like a lovely person in an undignified position yet confident none the less of being lovely.

F. Scott Fitzgerald | TENDER IS THE NIGHT | *1934*

PLATE FORTY-SIX: *La Boule de châtaigne* 1995

Solitaire

Extending an invitation is to assume responsibility for another's happiness for the entire time spent under one's roof.

| Anthelme Brillat-Savarin | LA PHYSIOLOGIE DU GOÛT | *1825* |

PLATE FORTY-SEVEN: *À table* 1997

Solitaire

I t was the best of times, it was the worst of times, it was the age of wisdom, it was the age of foolishness, it was the epoch of belief, it was the epoch of incredulity, it was the season of Light, it was the season of Darkness, it was the spring of hope, it was the winter of despair, we had everything before us, we had nothing before us . . .

| *Charles Dickens* | A TALE OF TWO CITIES | *1859* |

PLATE FORTY-EIGHT: *Deux Fenêtres, deux vies* 1987

Solitaire

The sight of the Luxembourg pathways made my heart jump; all other thoughts vanished. How many times, playing truant amid these knolls, I had stretched out in the shade, filled with wild poetry. Alas! This was the scene of my errant childhood ways. Among the leafless trees and spent plants of the flower-beds I found all these memories again. There, when I was ten, I had walked with my brother and my tutor, throwing bread to a few poor birds that were numb with cold; there, sitting in a corner, I watched for hours little girls dancing in a ring and listened to my naive heart beating to the refrains of their simple songs; there, coming home from school, I had crossed the same avenue countless times, kicking a pebble, lost in a line from Virgil. "Oh, my childhood!" I cried. "There you are. Oh, my God! There you are in this place!"

Alfred de Musset

LA CONFESSION D'UN ENFANT DU SIÈCLE

1836

PLATE FORTY-NINE: *La Chaise au Luxembourg* 1995

Solitaire

Alone, Rastignac stepped up to the heights of the cemetery to see Paris sinuously coiled along both banks of the Seine just as the evening lights were coming up. His eyes locked almost greedily on a place somewhere between Place Vendôme and the dome of Les Invalides, the very seat of the grand society he had so wanted to enter. He glared at this buzzing hive with a look that already seemed to drain it of its honey, and grandly vowed: "Now it's just the two of us."

And, as his first act of defiance toward society, Rastignac went to dine at the home of Lady Nucingen.

Honoré de Balzac	LE PÈRE GORIOT	*1835*

PLATE FIFTY: *Au Père-Lachaise* 1993

Credits

Translations from the French, unless otherwise noted, are by Jeff Kraft.

Page 22: Excerpt from "Paris in the Spring" from *The Big Sea* by Langston Hughes. Copyright © 1940 by Langston Hughes. Renewed copyright © 1968 by Arna Bontemps and George Houston Bass. Reprinted by permission of Hill and Wang, a division of Farrar, Straus & Giroux, Inc.

Page 24: Excerpt from *D'Après Paris* by Léon-Paul Fargue. Copyright © 1932 by Éditions Gallimard. Reprinted by permission.

Page 30: Excerpt from "The Eiffel Tower" from *The Eiffel Tower and Other Mythologies* by Roland Barthes, translated by Richard Howard. Translation copyright © 1979 by Farrar, Straus & Giroux, Inc. Reprinted by permission of Hill and Wang, a division of Farrar, Straus & Giroux, Inc.

Page 32: Excerpt from *Mémoires de Guerre: L'Appel* by Charles de Gaulle. Copyright © 1954 by Éditions Plon. Reprinted by permission of Librairie Plon.

Page 35: Excerpt from *Le Piéton de Paris* by Léon-Paul Fargue. Copyright © 1939 by Éditions Gallimard. Reprinted by permission.

Page 45: Excerpt from *The Early Diary of Anaïs Nin, Volume III: 1923-1927* by Anaïs Nin, copyright © 1983 by Rupert Pole as Trustee for the A. Nin Trust, reprinted by permission of Harcourt Brace & Company.

Pages 46, 97: Two excerpts from *The Notebooks of Malte Laurids Brigge* by Rainer Maria Rilke, translated by M.D. Herter Norton. Translation copyright © 1949 by W.W. Norton & Company, Inc., renewed © 1977 by M.D. Herter Norton Crena de Iongh. Reprinted by permission of W.W. Norton & Company, Inc.

Page 49: Excerpt from *To Myself* by Odilon Redon, translated by Mira Jacob and Jeanne L. Wassermann. Translation copyright © 1986 by George Braziller, Inc. Reprinted by permission.

Page 53: From *Giovanni's Room* by James Baldwin. Copyright © 1956 by James Baldwin. Used by permission of Doubleday, a division of Bantam Doubleday Dell Publishing Group, Inc.

Page 59: Excerpt from the 1951 song "Demain Il Fera Jour" by Marcel Achard and M. Monnot, as sung by Edith Piaf.

Page 62: Reprinted by permission of Scribner, a Division of Simon & Schuster, from *The Sun Also Rises* by Ernest Hemingway. Copyright © 1926 Charles Scribner's Sons. Copyright renewed © 1954 by Ernest Hemingway.

Page 65: From *Jean Rhys: The Complete Novels*. Copyright © 1985 by W.W. Norton & Company, Inc. Reprinted by permission of the Wallace Literary Agency, Inc.

Page 67: Excerpt from *Paris France* by Gertrude Stein. Copyright © 1940 by Charles Scribner's Sons. Reprinted by permission of Liveright Publishing Corporation.

Page 68: Excerpt from *Paroles* by Jacques Prévert. Copyright © 1948 by Éditions Gallimard. Reprinted by permission.

Page 74: Excerpt from *Pilote de Guerre* by Antoine de Saint-Exupéry, copyright © 1942 by Éditions Gallimard, reprinted by permission of Éditions Gallimard and Harcourt Brace & Company.

Page 81: Excerpt from *Paris Was Yesterday* by Janet Flanner. Copyright © 1972 by The Viking Press. Reprinted by permission of William Murray.

Page 82: Excerpt from *Le Paysan de Paris* by Louis Aragon. Copyright © 1926, renewed © 1953, by Éditions Gallimard. Reprinted by permission.

Page 89: Reprinted by permission of Scribner, a Division of Simon & Schuster, from *A Moveable Feast* by Ernest Hemingway. Copyright © 1964 by Mary Hemingway. Copyright renewed © 1992 by John H. Hemingway, Patrick Hemingway, and Gregory Hemingway.

Page 98: Excerpt from "The Eye of Paris" by Henry Miller, from *The Wisdom of the Heart*. Copyright © 1941 by New Directions Publishing Corp. Reprinted by permission of New Directions Publishing Corp.

Page 101: Excerpt from *Chéri* by Colette. Copyright © 1920 by Librairie Arthème Fayard. Reprinted by permission.

Page 103: Reprinted by permission of Scribner, a Division of Simon & Schuster, Inc. and Harold Ober Associates from *Tender Is the Night* by F. Scott Fitzgerald. Copyright © 1933, 1934 by Charles Scribner's Sons. Copyrights renewed © 1961, 1962 by Frances Scott Fitzgerald Lanahan.